Guided Reading an

PEARSON

Prentice
Hall

Boston, Massachusetts
Upper Saddle River, New Jersey

Copyright © by Pearson Education, Inc., publishing as Pearson Prentice Hall, Boston, Massachusetts 02116.
All rights reserved. Printed in the United States of America. This publication is protected by copyright, and permission should be obtained from the publisher prior to any prohibited reproduction, storage in a retrieval system, or transmission in any form or by any means, electronic, mechanical, photocopying, recording, or likewise. The publisher hereby grants permission to reproduce student worksheets and tests, for classroom use only, the number not to exceed the number of students in each class. Notice of copyright must appear on all copies. For information regarding permission(s), write to: Rights and Permissions Department, One Lake Street, Upper Saddle River, New Jersey 07458.

Pearson Prentice Hall™ is a trademark of Pearson Education, Inc.
Pearson® is a registered trademark of Pearson plc.
Prentice Hall® is a registered trademark of Pearson Education, Inc.

ISBN 0-13-190178-8   17 18 19 20 V011 16 15 14 13

Astronomy

Science Explorer • *Target Reading Skills Handbook*

Target Reading Skills

Identifying Main Ideas

Identifying the main idea helps you understand what you are reading. Sometimes the main idea can be easy to find. For example, suppose that you are reading just one paragraph. Very often you will find the main idea in the first sentence, the topic sentence. The other sentences in the paragraph provide supporting details or support the ideas in the topic sentence.

Sometimes, however, the first sentence is not the topic sentence. Sometimes you may have to look further. In those cases, it might help to read the paragraph and summarize what you have read. Your summary can give you the main idea.

A textbook has many paragraphs, each one with its own main idea. However, just as a paragraph has a main idea and supporting details, so does the text under each heading in your textbook. Sometimes the main idea is the heading itself. Other times it is more difficult to find. You may have to infer a main idea by combining information from several paragraphs.

To practice this skill, you can use a graphic organizer that looks like this one.

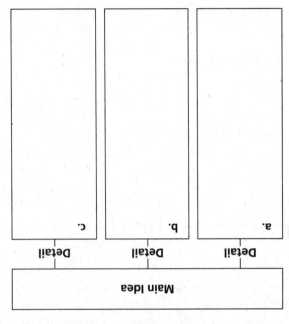

Outlining

Outlining shows you how supporting details relate to main ideas. You can make an outline as you read. Using this skill can make you a more careful reader.

Your outline can be made up of sentences, simple phrases, or single words. What matters is that you follow a formal structure. To outline while you read, use a plan like this one.

I. Section Title
  A. Main Heading
    1. Subheading
      a. Detail
      b. Detail
      c. Detail

The main ideas or topics are labeled as Roman numerals. The supporting details or subtopics are labeled A, B, C, and so on. Other levels of supporting information can be added under heads. When you outline in this way, you are deciding just how important a piece of information is.

Science Explorer ▪ *Target Reading Skills Handbook*

Comparing and Contrasting

You can use comparing and contrasting to better understand similarities and differences between two or more concepts. Look for clue words as you read. When concepts or topics are similar, you will probably see words such as *also, just as, like, likewise,* or *in the same way.* When concepts or topics are different, you will see *but, however, although, whereas, on the other hand,* or *unlike.*

To use this skill, it sometimes helps to make a Venn diagram. In this type of graphic organizer, the similarities are in the middle, where the two circles overlap.

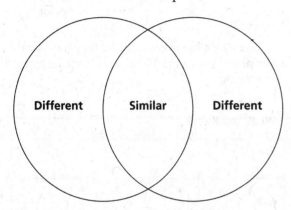

Relating Cause and Effect

Identifying causes and effects can help you understand the relationships among events. A cause is what makes something happen. An effect is what happens. In science, many actions cause other actions to occur.

Sometimes you have to look hard to see a cause-and-effect relationship in reading. You can watch for clue words to help you identify causes and effects. Look for *because, so, since, therefore, results, cause,* or *lead to.*

Sometimes a cause-and-effect relationship occurs in a chain. For example, an effect can have more than one cause, or a cause can have several effects. Seeing and understanding the relationships helps you understand science processes. You can use a graphic organizer like this one.

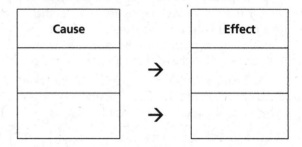

Asking Questions

Your textbook is organized using headings and subheadings. You can read the material under those headings by turning each heading into a question. For example, you might change the heading "Protecting Yourself During an Earthquake" to "How can you protect yourself during an earthquake?" Asking questions in this way will help you look for answers while reading. You can use a graphic organizer like this one to ask questions.

Question	Answer

Science Explorer ▪ *Target Reading Skills Handbook*

Sequencing

Sequencing is the order in which a series of events occurs. As you read, look for clue words that tell you the sequence or the order in which things happen. You see words such as *first, next, then,* or *finally.* When a process is being described, watch for numbered steps. Sometimes there are clues provided for you. Using the sequencing reading skill will help you understand and visualize the steps in a process. You can also use it to list events in the order of their occurrence.

You can use a graphic organizer to show the sequence of events or steps. The one most commonly used is a flowchart like this one.

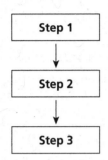

Sometimes, though, a cycle diagram works better.

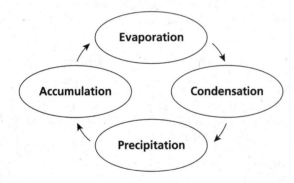

Using Prior Knowledge

Use prior knowledge to relate what you are reading to something that you already know. It is easier to learn when you can link new ideas to something that is already familiar to you. For example, if you know that fish are actually breathing oxygen that is dissolved in water, you wil be able to understand how or why gills work.

Using prior knowledge can help you make logical assumptions or draw conclusions about what you are reading. But be careful. Your prior knowledge might sometimes be wrong. As you read, you can confirm or correct your prior knowledge.

Use a graphic organizer like this one to link your prior knowledge to what you are learning as you read.

What You Know
1.
2.
3.

What You Learned
1.
2.
3.

Science Explorer ▪ *Target Reading Skills Handbook*

Previewing Visuals

Looking at visuals before you read can help you better understand a topic. Preview the visuals by reading labels and captions. For example, if you preview the visuals in a chapter about volcanoes, you will see more than just photographs of erupting volcanoes. You will see maps, diagrams, and photographs of rocks. These might tell you that you will learn where volcanoes are found, how they form, and what sort of rock is created when volcanoes erupt. Previewing visuals helps you understand and enjoy what you read.

One way to apply this strategy is to choose a few photographs, diagrams, or other visuals to preview. Then write questions about what you see. Answer the questions as you read.

Identifying Supporting Evidence

In science, you will read about hypotheses. A hypothesis is a possible explanation for scientific observations made by scientists or an answer to a scientific question. A hypothesis is tested over and over again. The tests may produce evidence that supports the hypothesis. When enough supporting evidence is collected, a hypothesis may become a theory.

Identifying supporting evidence in your reading can help you understand a hypothesis or theory. Evidence is made up of facts. Facts are information that can be confirmed by testing or observation.

When you are identifying supporting evidence, a graphic organizer like this one can be helpful.

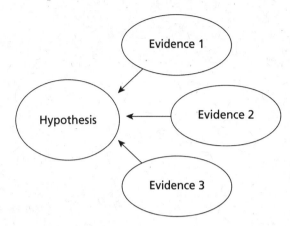

Building Vocabulary

To understand what someone is saying, you have to know the language that person is speaking. To understand science, you need to know what the words mean.

There are many ways to build your vocabulary. You can look up the meaning of a new word in a dictionary or glossary. Then you can write its definition in your own words. You can use the new word in a sentence. To figure out the meaning of a new word, you can use context clues or surrounding words. Look for prefixes and suffixes in the new word to help you break it down. Building vocabulary will get easier with practice.

Earth, Moon, and Sun • *Guided Reading and Study*

Earth in Space (pp. 7–13)

This section explains what causes day and night and what causes the cycle of seasons on Earth.

Use Target Reading Skills

As you read about seasons on Earth, stop and write what you know about that topic. As you read the passage, write what you learn.

What You Know
1. The sun's rays heat Earth.
2.
3.
4.

What You Learned
1.
2.
3.
4.

Introduction (p. 6)

1. The study of the moon, stars, and other objects in space is called

   _____ .

Earth, Moon, and Sun • *Guided Reading and Study*

Earth in Space *(continued)*

How Earth Moves (pp. 7–9)

Match the term with its definition.

Term	Definition
_____ 2. axis	**a.** The movement of one object around another object
_____ 3. rotation	**b.** The imaginary line that passes through Earth's center and the North and South poles
_____ 4. revolution	**c.** The path of an object as it revolves around another object in space
_____ 5. orbit	**d.** The spinning motion of Earth on its axis

6. What causes day and night?

   _____

   _____

7. Each 24-hour cycle of day and night is called a(n) _____.

8. Why is an extra day added to February every four years?

   _____

   _____

   _____

   _____

   _____

The Seasons on Earth (pp. 10–13)

9. Why is it warmer near the equator than near the poles?

   _____

   _____

   _____

   _____

10. Why does Earth have seasons?

    _____

    _____

    _____

Earth, Moon, and Sun • *Guided Reading and Study*

11. Circle the letter of each sentence that is true.

   a. Earth is closest to the sun when it is summer in the Northern Hemisphere.

   b. The hemisphere that is tilted away from the sun has more daylight than the other hemisphere.

   c. When it is summer in the Northern Hemisphere it is winter in the Southern Hemisphere.

   d. In June, there are fewer hours of daylight and less direct sunlight in the Southern Hemisphere.

12. Each of the two days of the year when the noon sun is farthest north or south of the equator is called a(n) _____.

13. Each of the two days of the year when neither hemisphere is tilted toward or away from the sun is called a(n) _____.

14. Complete the table to show the relationship of Earth's tilt to the seasons in the Northern Hemisphere.

Earth's Seasons in the Northern Hemisphere			
Day in Northern Hemisphere	**Approximate Date Each Year**	**Length of Daytime**	**Hemisphere That Is Tilted Toward the Sun**
Summer solstice	a.	Longest daytime	b.
Autumnal equinox	c.	d.	Neither
Winter solstice	December 21	e.	f.
Vernal equinox	g.	Daytime equals nighttime	h.

15. Use the table to circle the letters of the statements that are true about Earth's seasons in the Northern Hemisphere.

   a. When the Northern Hemisphere has summer, the Southern Hemisphere is tilted away from the sun.

   b. In December, the shortest daytime is in the Southern Hemisphere.

   c. The autumnal equinox falls on September 22 to mark the beginning of fall in both hemispheres.

   d. An equinox occurs on the same days at the same time in both hemispheres.

Earth, Moon, and Sun • *Guided Reading and Study*

Gravity and Motion (pp. 16–19)

This section describes the two factors that keep the planets in orbit around the sun and moons in orbit around planets.

Use Target Reading Skills

Complete the first column in the chart by previewing the red headings and asking a what, how, or where question for each. As you read the section, complete the second column with the answers. The first question is done for you. Answer that question, and then think of another one about gravity.

Question	Answer
What is gravity?	a. Gravity is
b. (Gravity)	c.
d. (Inertia and Orbital Motion)	e.

Gravity (pp. 16–17)

1. Is the following statement true or false? Forces on Earth are different from those elsewhere in the universe. _____

2. What is the law of universal gravitation?

   _____

   _____

3. What two factors determine the strength of the force of gravity between two objects?

   a._____

   b._____

Earth, Moon, and Sun · *Guided Reading and Study*

4. Complete the cause and effect table to show the relationship among mass, distance, and the force of gravity between two objects.

CAUSE		EFFECT
If mass	*and distance*	*then the force of gravity between two objects*
increases	stays the same	**a.**
b.	stays the same	decreases.
stays the same	decreases	**c.**
stays the same	increases	**d.**

e. Use the information in the table to write one or two sentences about the relationship among mass, distance, and the force of gravity between two objects.

_____

_____

_____

_____

Inertia and Orbital Motion (pp. 18–19)

5. What is inertia?

_____

_____

_____

6. Isaac Newton concluded that two factors combined to keep the planets in orbit. Name them.

a._____

b._____

7. Circle the letter of each statement that is true about the moon's orbit around Earth.

   a. Earth's gravity pulls the moon toward it.
   b. The moon keeps moving ahead because of gravity.
   c. The moon would stop moving if Earth's gravity did not pull on it.
   d. Inertia keeps the moon moving ahead.

Earth, Moon, and Sun • *Guided Reading and Study*

Phases, Eclipses, and Tides (pp. 20–27)

This section explains what causes phases of the moon, what causes eclipses, and what causes the tides.

Use Target Reading Skills

Look at the Figure "Phases of the Moon" in your text. In the graphic organizer below, write a second question you have about the visuals. As you read about the moon, write the answers to both questions.

Q. Why does the moon have phases?
A.
Q.
A.

Motions of the Moon (p. 20)

1. Circle the letter of each sentence that is true about motions of the moon.

   a. The moon revolves around Earth once a year.
   b. The same side of the moon always faces Earth.
   c. The moon rotates slowly on its axis once every 27.3 days.
   d. A "day" and a "year" on the moon are the same length.

2. What causes the phases of the moon, eclipses, and tides?

   _____

   _____

Phases of the Moon (pp. 21–23)

3. The different shapes of the moon you see from Earth are called

   _____.

4. How often does the moon go through an entire set of phases?

   _____

   _____

Earth, Moon, and Sun • *Guided Reading and Study*

5. What does the phase of the moon you see depend on?

   _____

   _____

   _____

6. Complete the table to show what you see during the different phases of the moon.

Phases of the Moon	
Phase	**What You See**
New moon	The side of the moon facing Earth is dark.
First quarter	a.
Full moon	b.
Third quarter	c.

   d. Is the near side (facing Earth) always the dark side? Use the table to explain your answer.

   _____

   _____

   _____

   e. What percentage of the dark side of the moon do you see during the first and third quarters?

   _____

Earth, Moon, and Sun • *Guided Reading and Study*

Phases, Eclipses, and Tides (continued)

Eclipses (pp. 23–25)

7. When the moon's shadow hits Earth or Earth's shadow hits the moon, what occurs?

   _____

8. What are the two types of eclipses?

   a. _____ b. _____

9. The darkest part of the moon's shadow is called the

   _____ .

10. What causes a solar eclipse?

    _____

    _____

    _____

11. The larger part of a shadow, less dark than the umbra, is called the

    _____.

12. Circle the letter of each sentence that is true about solar eclipses.
    a. People in the umbra see only a partial solar eclipse.
    b. During a partial solar eclipse, part of the sun remains visible.
    c. During a total solar eclipse, the sky grows dark.
    d. People in the penumbra see a total solar eclipse.

13. What is the arrangement of Earth, the moon, and the sun during a lunar eclipse?

    _____

    _____

14. Circle the letter of each sentence that is true about lunar eclipses.
    a. People see a total lunar eclipse when the moon is in Earth's penumbra.
    b. A lunar eclipse always occurs at a full moon.
    c. During a lunar eclipse, Earth blocks sunlight from reaching the moon.
    d. A partial lunar eclipse occurs when the moon passes partly into the umbra of Earth's shadow.

Earth, Moon, and Sun ▪ *Guided Reading and Study*

Tides (pp. 26–27)

15. The rise and fall of ocean water are called _____.

16. What force pulls the moon and Earth toward each other?
_____

17. Why do tides occur?

_____

_____

_____

18. Circle the letter of each sentence that is true about tides.

    a. The point on Earth that is closest to the moon has a high tide.

    b. Every location on Earth has two high tides per month.

    c. A low tide occurs at the point on Earth farthest from the moon.

    d. The point on Earth farthest from the moon has a high tide.

19. What is a spring tide?

_____

_____

20. What is a neap tide?

_____

_____

21. On the illustrations below, draw the possible position(s) of the moon at spring tide and at neap tide.

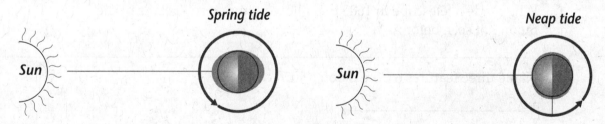

Spring tide   Neap tide

Sun   Sun

22. Circle the letter of each of the phases of the moon when it is possible for a spring tide to occur.

    a. new moon

    b. first quarter

    c. full moon

    d. third quarter

Earth, Moon, and Sun ▪ *Guided Reading and Study*

Earth's Moon (pp. 30–33)

This section describes the features of the moon that can be seen with a telescope. It also describes the characteristics and origin of the moon.

Use Target Reading Skills

As you read about the moon's surface, fill in the detail boxes that explain the main idea in the graphic organizer below.

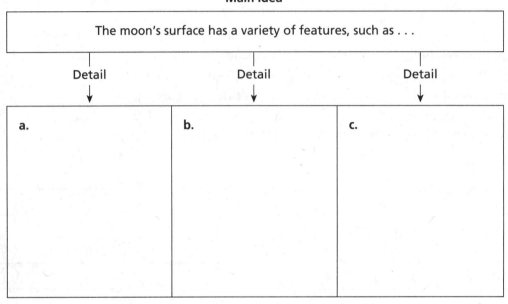

Main Idea

The moon's surface has a variety of features, such as . . .

Detail   Detail   Detail

a.   b.   c.

The Moon's Surface (p. 31)

1. Who made a telescope in 1609 that allowed him to see details of the moon not seen before?

   _____

2. Name three features on the moon's surface.

   a. _____

   b. _____

   c. _____

3. Round pits on the surface of the moon are called

   _____.

4. What are craters on the moon caused by?

   _____

   _____

   _____

Name _____ Date _____ Class _____

5. Circle the letter of the phrase that best describes maria.
   a. highland peaks that cast dark shadows
   b. dark, flat areas that were formed by huge lava flows
   c. vast oceans that cover much of the moon
   d. craters made from exploded volcanoes

6. How did Galileo infer that the moon has highlands?

   _____

   _____

   _____

Characteristics of the Moon (p. 32)

7. Circle the letter of the relative diameter of the moon.
   a. about twice the size of Earth
   b. about half Earth's diameter
   c. about the distance across the United States, including Hawaii
   d. about one quarter Earth's diameter

8. Is the following statement true or false? The moon's average density is similar to the density of Earth's core. _____

9. Why do temperatures on the moon vary so much?

   _____

   _____

   _____

   _____

10. There is evidence that the moon has ice. Explain where the ice is thought to exist and why it remains frozen.

   _____

   _____

   _____

   _____

Earth, Moon, and Sun • *Guided Reading and Study*

Earth's Moon *(continued)*

The Origin of the Moon (p. 33)

11. Complete the flowchart to show the sequence of events in the collision-ring theory.

The Collision-Ring Theory

A large object collided with **a.** _____

↓

Material from **b.** _____ outer layer was ejected into space.

↓

The material from Earth was thrown into **c.** _____ and formed a ring.

↓

Gravity caused this material to form the **d.** _____ .

e. Use the flowchart to summarize in your own words how the moon was formed.

_____

_____

_____

_____

Earth, Moon, and Sun · *Key Terms*

Key Terms

The hidden-word puzzle below contains 12 key terms from the chapter. You might find them across, down, or on the diagonal. Use the clues to identify the hidden terms. Then circle each term in the puzzle.

Clues   **Key Terms**

1. The spinning motion of Earth around its axis   _____

2. The study of the moon, stars, and other objects in space _____

3. The different shapes of the moon you see from Earth   _____

4. The imaginary line that passes through Earth's center and the North and South poles   _____

5. The two days of the year on which the sun reaches its greatest distance north or south of the equator   _____

6. Earth's path as it revolves around the sun   _____

7. The movement of one object around another object   _____

8. The cyclical rise or fall of ocean water   _____

9. A round pit on the moon's surface   _____

10. The darkest part of the moon's shadow   _____

11. Dark, flat areas on the moon's surface   _____

12. The part of a shadow that surrounds the darkest part   _____

```
x   c   r   a   t   e   r   r   u   q   r
p   a   s   t   r   o   n   o   m   y   e
e   x   o   m   o   n   t   t   b   w   v
n   i   l   m   a   r   i   a   r   l   o
u   s   s   d   e   n   b   t   a   t   l
m   w   t   d   c   m   s   i   m   i   u
b   s   i   k   p   m   b   o   t   a   t
r   t   c   m   l   s   s   n   p   t   i
a   a   e   u   i   l   k   a   i   d   o
y   p   h   a   s   e   s   h   n   u   n
```

Exploring Space • *Guided Reading and Study*

The Science of Rockets (pp. 40–45)

This section explains how rockets were developed and how they work.

Use Target Reading Skills

Before you read about rockets, write what you know about them in the box "What You Know." As you read the section, complete the "What You Learned" box.

What You Know
1. Rockets were used to help transport astronauts to the moon. 2. 3. 4.

What You Learned
1. 2. 3. 4.

A History of Rockets (p. 41)

1. Rocket technology originated in
   a. China.
   b. Russia.
   c. the United States.
   d. Germany.

2. When were modern rockets first developed?

_____

_____

Exploring Space · *Guided Reading and Study*

3. Rank the following events in the history of rockets from earliest in time to latest in time. Rank the earliest event as 1.

_____ The British used rockets against American troops.

_____ Rockets carried explosives during World War II.

_____ The Chinese coated arrows with a flammable powder.

_____ Rockets launched astronauts to the moon.

_____ The Chinese used gunpowder inside their rockets.

_____ Scientists such as Goddard first designed and tested modern rockets.

4. Describe the contribution of the German scientist von Braun to the U.S. space program.

_____

_____

_____

How Do Rockets Work? (pp. 42–43)

5. Why does a rocket move forward?

_____

_____

6. For every force, or action, there is an equal and opposite force, or

_____.

7. Circle the letter of each sentence that is true about velocity, orbital velocity, or escape velocity.

   a. A rocket must move faster than orbital velocity to establish an orbit.
   b. The force that propels a rocket forward is its velocity.
   c. A rocket must reach escape velocity to leave Earth's orbit.
   d. Escape velocity is greater than orbital velocity.

8. What are the three main types of rockets that power modern spacecraft?

   a. _____

   b. _____

   c. _____

Exploring Space ▪ *Guided Reading and Study*

The Science of Rockets (continued)

Multistage Rockets (pp. 44–45)

9. What happens to the first stage of a multistage rocket?

   _____

10. What happens to the second stage when the first stage uses up its fuel?

   _____

11. Complete the flowchart to show the sequence of events in a multistage rocket.

   ┌───┐
   │ **1.** Heavy first stage provides thrust for launch.   │
   └───┘
                                  ↓
   ┌───┐
   │ **2.** First stage separates and **a.** _____ .   │
   └───┘
                                  ↓
   ┌───┐
   │ **3. b.** _____ stage ignites and continues moving with third stage. │
   └───┘
                                  ↓
   ┌───┐
   │ **4.** Second stage **c.** _____ and falls to Earth. │
   └───┘
                                  ↓
   ┌───┐
   │ **5.** Third stage **d.** _____ .   │
   └───┘
                                  ↓
   ┌───┐
   │ **6.** Rocket reaches its destination.   │
   └───┘

12. What is the main advantage of a multistage rocket?

   _____

   _____

13. What did the development of multistage rockets make possible?

   _____

   _____

Exploring Space ▪ *Guided Reading and Study*

The Space Program (pp. 48–52)

This section describes the space race and missions to the moon.

Use Target Reading Skills

Complete the first column in the chart by previewing the red headings and asking a what, how, or where question for each. As you read the section, complete the second column with the answers. The first question is done for you.

Question	Answer
What was the "space race"?	

The Race for Space (pp. 48–49)

1. Circle the letter of the first artificial satellite launched into space.

   a. *Skylab*   c. *Sputnik I*
   b. *Explorer 1*   d. *Mir*

2. What is a satellite?

   _____

   _____

   _____

3. How did the United States respond to the launch of the first artificial satellite by the Soviet Union?

   _____

   _____

   _____

4. What was the name of the first satellite launched by the United States?

   _____

   _____

Exploring Space ▪ *Guided Reading and Study*

The Space Program *(continued)*

5. Is the following statement true or false? The first American in space was John Glenn. _____

6. Complete the following table of major events in the space race.

Year	Event
1957	The Soviet Union launched **a.** _____
b. _____	The **c.** _____ launched *Explorer I*.
1961	The **d.** _____ launched the first human in space.
e. _____	An astronaut named **f.** _____ became the first American in space.

g. Use the table above to write an explanation in your own words of how these events illustrate the meaning of "space race."

_____

_____

_____

_____

_____

Missions to the Moon (pp. 50–52)

7. What was the Apollo program, and who started it?

_____

_____

_____

8. Circle the letter of the spacecraft that transported the first astronauts to land on the moon in July 1969.

   a. *Surveyor*   **c.** *Skylab*

   b. *Sputnik I*   **d.** *Apollo 11*

Exploring Space • *Guided Reading and Study*

9. Who was the first person to walk on the moon?

_____

_____

10. Who said the first words spoken on the moon, and what were the words?

_____

_____

_____

11. Circle the letter of each statement that is true about the Apollo missions.

    a. The first astronaut to walk on the moon landed on the moon in 1964.

    b. Astronauts used lunar rovers to explore the moon's surface.

    c. The Apollo missions continued from the 1960s until the 1990s.

    d. Apollo astronauts contributed to our knowledge of the moon's structure.

12. What are moon rocks?

_____

_____

13. How are moon rocks similar to and different from rocks on Earth?

_____

_____

_____

_____

14. What did scientists learn from creating artificial moonquakes?

_____

_____

_____

15. Is the following sentence true or false? The moon has natural moonquakes that are weaker than earthquakes on Earth. _____

16. What is one reason for recent renewed interest in the moon?

_____

_____

_____

Exploring Space Today (pp. 53–57)

This section explains the roles of space shuttles, space stations, and space probes.

Use Target Reading Skills

As you read about exploring space today, complete the outline to show the relationships among the headings.

Exploring Space Today
I. Working in space
A. Space shuttles
B.
II. Space probes
A.
B.

Working in Space (pp. 54–55)

1. What is a space shuttle?

   _____

2. List three tasks that space shuttles perform.

   a. _____

   b. _____

   c. _____

3. A large artificial satellite in which people can live for long periods is called a(n) _____.

4. Circle the letter of each statement that is true about space stations.
   a. The main power source of the International Space Station is solar cells.
   b. The International Space Station was completed in 1998.
   c. A space station is a large artificial satellite on which people can live and work for long periods.
   d. The Soviet space station *Mir* is currently orbiting Earth.

Space Probes (pp. 56–57)

Match the space probe with the primary planet(s) or moon(s) that it explored.

	Space Probe		Planet or Moon
____	5. *Galileo*	a.	Mars
____	6. *Lunar Prospector*	b.	Saturn and Titan
____	7. *Opportunity*	c.	Jupiter and its moons
____	8. *Cassini*	d.	Earth's moon

9. Complete the table to compare and contrast space shuttles, space stations, and space probes.

	Spacecraft		
Feature	Space Shuttle	Space Station	Space Probe
Carry/Support Humans	Yes	a.	b.
Purpose	Transport people and equipment	c.	d.
Source of Power	e.	f.	Onboard system to produce electricity

g. Which type of spacecraft is best suited to explore planets that have very different conditions from those of Earth? Why?

_____

_____

_____

h. The International Space Station operates by a renewable energy source—one that will not run out. Why is this important?

_____

_____

_____

Exploring Space ▪ *Guided Reading and Study*

Using Space Science on Earth (pp. 58–62)

This section describes how conditions in space differ from those on Earth, the benefits of space technology for society, and the uses of satellites orbiting Earth.

Use Target Reading Skills

As you read about space spinoffs, fill in the detail boxes that explain the main idea in the graphic organizer below.

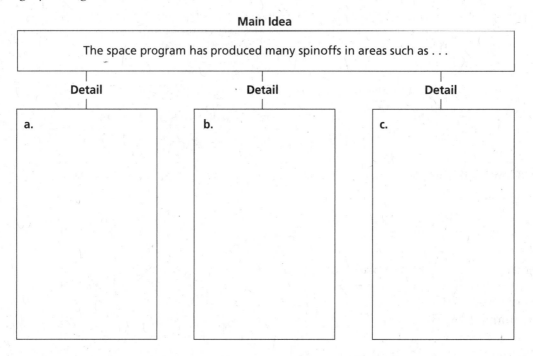

Main Idea

The space program has produced many spinoffs in areas such as . . .

Detail	Detail	Detail
a.	b.	c.

The Challenges of Space (p. 59)

1. List three conditions in space that differ from those on Earth.

   a. _____

   b. _____

   c. _____

2. A place that is empty of all matter is a(n) _____.

3. Is the following statement true or false? In space, temperatures are extreme because there is no air. _____

4. a. Why does an astronaut experience a feeling of weightlessness in orbit?

   _____

   _____

   _____

   b. What is this condition called?

   _____

Space Spinoffs (pp. 60–61)

5. An item that has uses on Earth but was developed for space is called a(n)

_____.

6. What are three examples of medical spinoffs from the space program?

   a. _____

   b. _____

   c. _____

Match the materials or devices used in space with the item in which they are used on Earth.

Use in Space	Use on Earth
____ 7. Batteries for space power systems	a. athletic shoes
____ 8. Lightweight spacecraft components	b. tennis rackets
____ 9. Astronauts' moon boots	c. video games
____ 10. Insulation against radiation	d. pacemakers
____ 11. Lunar rover operation	e. insulation for houses

Satellites (p. 62)

12. Name three ways that satellites are used for communications.

   a. _____

   _____

   b. _____

   _____

   c. _____

   _____

13. What does it mean for a satellite to be in geosynchronous orbit?

_____

_____

14. Circle the letter of each sentence that is true about satellites.

   a. Most communications satellites are placed in a geosynchronous orbit.
   b. In remote sensing, a satellite must directly contact Earth.
   c. Satellites can collect data on conditions above, at, and below Earth's surface.
   d. Satellites are being replaced by computers that produce images from data.

Exploring Space · *Key Terms*

Key Terms

Match each definition in the left column with the correct term in the right column. Then write the number of each term in the appropriate box below. When you have filled all the boxes, add the numbers in each column and row. All of the sums should be the same.

Definitions

A. the reaction force that propels a rocket forward

B. a device that expels gas in one direction to move in the opposite direction

C. a place that is empty of all matter

D. speed in a given direction

E. a large artificial satellite in which people live and work

F. indirectly acquiring information about Earth's surface

G. an item used on Earth, but developed for use in space

H. spacecraft that has scientific instruments but no human crew

I. the velocity a rocket must achieve to establish an orbit

Terms

1. velocity
2. space probe
3. vacuum
4. rocket
5. remote sensing
6. space spinoff
7. orbital velocity
8. thrust
9. space station

A	B	C
___	___	___
D	E	F
___	___	___
G	H	I
___	___	___

___ = ___ = ___

The Solar System • *Guided Reading and Study*

Observing the Solar System (pp. 72–77)

This section describes the history of ideas about the solar system.

Use Target Reading Skills

Look at Figures 2 and 3 in your textbook, and write two questions about the visuals in the graphic organizer below. The first question is done for you. As you read, write the answers to your questions.

Q. What is a geocentric model?
A.
Q.
A.

Earth at the Center (p. 73)

1. What did the Romans name the points of light that the Greeks called planets?

   _____

   _____

2. In a geocentric system, what is at the center of the universe?

   _____

   _____

3. How was Ptolemy's model different from the earlier Greek model?

   _____

   _____

   _____

The Solar System • *Guided Reading and Study*

Observing the Solar System *(continued)*

Sun at the Center (pp. 74–75)

4. A description of the solar system in which all the planets revolve around the sun is called a(n) _____ .

5. In the 1500s, who further developed the heliocentric explanation for the motion of the planets?

    _____

6. What were two observations that Galileo made through his telescope that supported the heliocentric model?

    _____

    _____

    _____

    _____

7. Circle the letter next to the name of the person or group whose ideas about the solar system are largely accepted today.
    a. Copernicus
    b. the people of ancient Greece
    c. Ptolemy
    d. the Romans

8. What is an ellipse?

    _____

    _____

The Solar System ▪ *Guided Reading and Study*

9. Complete the table below, which shows what each scientist contributed to our knowledge of the solar system.

Observer	Time	Accomplishment
Copernicus	a.	Further developed heliocentric model; worked out arrangement of known planets
Brahe	Late 1500s	b.
c.	d.	Used a telescope to make discoveries that supported the heliocentric model
Kepler	Early 1600s	e.

f. Use the table to give examples of how the work of many scientists over time has led to our current understanding of the solar system.

_____

_____

_____

Modern Discoveries (pp. 76–77)

10. What does the solar system consist of?

_____

_____

_____

The Solar System · *Guided Reading and Study*

The Sun (pp. 78–82)

This section describes the sun's interior and its atmosphere. It also describes features on and above the sun's surface.

Use Target Reading Skills

As you read about the sun, complete the outline to show the relationships among the headings.

The Sun
I. The Sun's Interior

_____

_____

_____

II. _____

_____

   B. The Chromosphere

_____

III. _____

_____

_____

   C. Solar Flares

_____

The Sun's Interior (p. 79)

1. The sun's energy comes from a process called
   _____.

2. What occurs in nuclear fusion?

   _____

   _____

3. Where does nuclear fusion occur in the sun?

   _____

   _____

4. Order the layers of the sun's interior from inner layer to outer layer.

   _____

   _____

The Solar System · *Guided Reading and Study*

The Sun's Atmosphere (p. 80)

5. Order the layers of the sun's atmosphere from inner layer to outer layer.
_____

6. Which layer do you see when you look at a typical image of the sun?
_____

7. How can you identify the chromosphere during a total solar eclipse?
_____

8. Why can you see a corona during a total solar eclipse?
_____
_____

9. The corona sends out a stream of electrically charged particles called the
_____.

Features on the Sun (pp. 80–82)

10. Name three features on or above the sun's surface.

    a. _____   b. _____

    c. _____

Match the feature on the sun with its description.

Feature	Description
____ 11. sunspots	a. Areas of gas on the sun's surface that are cooler than the gases around them
____ 12. prominences	b. Large eruptions of gas out into space
____ 13. solar flares	c. Reddish loops of gas that link different parts of sunspot regions

14. When solar flares increase solar wind from the corona, what do they cause in Earth's upper atmosphere? _____

The Solar System • *Guided Reading and Study*

The Inner Planets (pp. 84–91)

This section describes the main characteristics of the four planets closest to the sun.

Use Target Reading Skills

As you come to each major head in the section, stop and write what you know about that topic. As you read the passage, write what you learn.

What You Know
1. Most of Earth is covered with water.
2.
3.
4.

What You Learned
1.
2.
3.
4.

Introduction (p. 84)

1. Which planets are often called the terrestrial planets?

   _____

   _____

2. What are three similarities among the inner planets?

   _____

   _____

Name _____ Date _____ Class _____

Use the table "The Inner Planets" in your textbook to answer questions 3 and 4.

3. Rank the inner planets according to diameter. Rank the planet with the greatest diameter as *1*.

    _____ Mercury _____ Venus _____ Earth _____ Mars

4. Which planet rotates on its axis in about the same amount of time that Earth does? _____

5. The drawing below shows the sun and the four inner planets. Label the inner planets according to their place in the solar system.

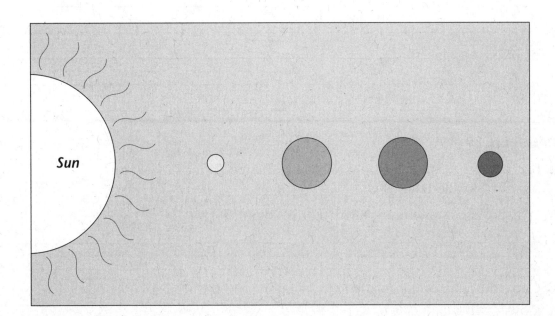

Earth (pp. 84–85)

6. Circle the letter of each sentence that is true about Earth.

    a. About 70 percent of its surface is covered with water.
    b. Its atmosphere extends about 1 kilometer above its surface.
    c. Most of the atmosphere is composed of oxygen gas.
    d. No other planet in the solar system has oceans like Earth's.

7. What are the three main layers of Earth?

    a. _____   b. _____

    c. _____

8. What is Earth's dense inner core made of? _____

The Solar System • *Guided Reading and Study*

The Inner Planets *(continued)*

Mercury (p. 86)

9. Circle the letter of each sentence that is true about Mercury.

   a. Mercury's surface has many craters.
   b. Mercury has no moons.
   c. The interior of Mercury is composed mostly of the element mercury.
   d. Mercury is the planet closest to the sun.

10. Why does Mercury have a greater range of temperatures than any other planet?

    _____
    _____
    _____
    _____
    _____

Venus (pp. 87–88)

11. Because Venus is often a bright object in the west after sunset, it is sometimes called the _____.

12. Why is Venus sometimes called "Earth's twin"?

    _____
    _____

13. Circle the letter of the gas that makes up most of the atmosphere of the planet Venus.

    a. oxygen
    b. nitrogen
    c. sulfuric acid
    d. carbon dioxide

14. How is the rotation of Venus different from that of most other planets and moons?

    _____
    _____
    _____

15. Is the following sentence true or false? The atmosphere of Venus is so thick that there is never a sunny day on its surface.

    _____

16. The trapping of heat by the atmosphere of Venus is called the _____.

The Solar System ▪ *Guided Reading and Study*

Mars (pp. 89–91)

17. Why is Mars called the "red planet"?

_____

_____

_____

18. The atmosphere on Mars is composed mostly of

_____.

19. Is the following sentence true or false? There are no canals on Mars.

_____

20. Why do some regions on Mars look darker than others?

_____

_____

_____

21. Circle the letter of each sentence that is true about Mars.
   a. Mars' polar ice caps contain frozen water and carbon dioxide.
   b. Mars has seasons because it is tilted on its axis.
   c. Mars has many large oceans on its surface.
   d. Mars has giant volcanoes on its surface.

22. What are the two moons of Mars?

   a. _____   **b.** _____

23. Complete the table to compare and contrast characteristics of Earth and Mars.

Characteristics of Earth and Mars		
Characteristic	**Earth**	**Mars**
Atmosphere	Mostly nitrogen and oxygen	**a.**
Moons	One	**b.**
Seasons	**c.**	Yes
Surface	Solid and rocky	**d.**
Water	**e.**	At poles and possibly underground

   f. Use the table to identify which characteristics of Mars make it difficult or impossible for humans to live there without life support.

_____

_____

The Solar System • *Guided Reading and Study*

The Outer Planets

This section describes the main characteristics of the four planets farthest from the sun. It also explains how Pluto is different from the planets.

Use Target Reading Skills

As you read about the similarities among the gas giants, fill in the detail boxes that explain the main idea in the graphic organizer below.

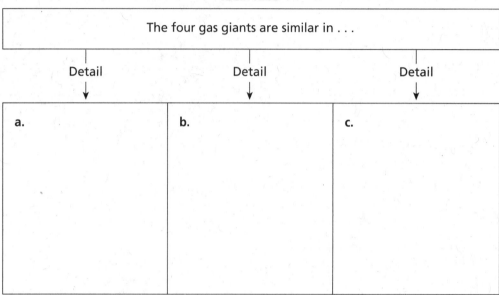

Main Idea

The four gas giants are similar in . . .

Detail | Detail | Detail

a. | b. | c.

Gas Giants and Pluto

1. The four outer planets do not have solid _____.

2. Which four planets are known as the gas giants?

   _____

   _____

3. What is the composition of the gas giants?

   _____

   _____

   _____

The Solar System • *Guided Reading and Study*

4. The drawing below shows the sun, the four inner planets, the four outer planets, and Pluto. Label the outer planets and Pluto according to their typical place in the solar system.

5. Describe the composition of the rings that surround the gas giants.

_____

_____

Jupiter

6. Is the following sentence true or false? Jupiter is the most massive planet in the solar system. _____

7. What is the Great Red Spot on Jupiter?

_____

_____

_____

8. Circle the letter of each sentence that is true about Jupiter.

   a. Jupiter has a dense core of hydrogen and helium.
   b. Jupiter's atmosphere is extremely thin.
   c. Jupiter has dozens of moons revolving around it.
   d. Many of Jupiter's moons have been discovered in recent years.

9. What are Jupiter's four largest moons?

   a. _____   **b.** _____

   c. _____   **d.** _____

10. Jupiter's moon Io is covered with active _____.

The Solar System • *Guided Reading and Study*

The Outer Planets *(continued)*

Saturn (p. 98)

11. What are Saturn's rings made of?

_____

_____

_____

12. Is the following sentence true or false? Saturn has only a few moons.

_____

13. The largest of Saturn's moons is called _____.

Uranus (p. 99)

14. Why does Uranus look blue-green?

_____

_____

15. How much larger is Uranus than Earth?

_____

16. What discovery made astronomer William Herschel famous?

_____

_____

_____

17. How is the rotation of Uranus unlike that of most of the other planets?

_____

_____

_____

18. What are Uranus's five largest moons like?

_____

_____

_____

19. Which spacecraft sent many images of Uranus back to Earth?

_____

The Solar System • *Guided Reading and Study*

Neptune

20. Is the following sentence true or false? Neptune's atmosphere is yellow and has no clouds. _____

21. In the 1800s, how did astronomers predict that the planet Neptune would be discovered before anyone had seen it?

   _____

   _____

   _____

   _____

22. Circle the letter of the sentence that explains how the Great Dark Spot was like the Great Red Spot.

   a. Both formed from volcanoes.
   b. Both formed on rings.
   c. Both were probably storms.
   d. Neither lasted long.

23. Which is the largest of Neptune's moons? _____

Pluto

24. Is the following sentence true or false? Pluto is smaller than Earth's moon. _____

25. How often does Pluto revolve around the sun?

   _____

   _____

26. Circle the letter of each sentence that is true about Pluto.

   a. Charon is more than half Pluto's size.
   b. Pluto has a gaseous surface.
   c. Pluto is no longer considered to be a planet.
   d. Pluto is sometimes closer to the sun than Neptune.

27. How is a dwarf planet similar to and different from a planet?

   _____

   _____

   _____

   _____

The Solar System • *Guided Reading and Study*

Comets, Asteroids, and Meteors (pp. 104–107)

This section describes the other objects in the solar system, including comets, asteroids, and meteors.

Use Target Reading Skills

As you read about comets, asteroids, and meteoroids, fill in the graphic organizer below to compare and contrast their origin, size, and composition.

Feature	Comets	Asteroids	Meteoroids
Origin	Kuiper belt and Oort cloud	a.	b.
Size	c.	d.	Smaller than comets or asteroids
Composition	e.	Rock	f.

Comets (p. 105)

1. What are comets?

   _____

   _____

   _____

2. What are the three main parts of a comet?

   a. _____   b. _____

   c. _____

3. What forms a comet's tail?

   _____

   _____

4. Is the following sentence true or false? A comet's tail can be more than 100 million kilometers long. _____

5. If the orbit of a comet is 500 times the distance between Pluto and the sun, which region is it in? Explain how you know.

_____

_____

_____

_____

_____

Asteroids (p. 106)

6. Rocky objects revolving around the sun that are too small and too numerous to be called planets are called _____.

7. Where is the asteroid belt?

_____

_____

8. What happened when an asteroid collided with Earth 65 million years ago?

_____

_____

_____

_____

Meteors (p. 107)

Match the term with its definition.

Term	Definition
____ 9. meteoroid	**a.** A meteoroid that has passed through the atmosphere and hit Earth's surface
____ 10. meteor	**b.** A chunk of rock or dust in space
____ 11. meteorite	**c.** A streak of light caused by the burning up of a meteoroid in the atmosphere

12. Where do meteoroids come from?

_____

_____

13. The craters on the moon were caused by the impact of

_____.

The Solar System · *Guided Reading and Study*

Is There Life Beyond Earth? (pp. 108–111)

This section describes what conditions living things need to exist on Earth and explains why life might exist on Mars and Europa.

Use Target Reading Skills

Complete the first column in the chart by previewing the red headings in your textbook and asking a what, how, *or* where *question for each. As you read the section, complete the second column with the answers. The first question is done for you.*

Question	Answer
What are the "Goldilocks" conditions?	a.
b.	c.

Introduction (p. 108)

1. Life other than that on Earth would be called

_____

Life on Earth (p. 109)

2. What are the three "Goldilocks conditions" on Earth that life as we know it must have to exist?

    a. _____

    b. _____

    c. _____

Name _____ Date _____ Class _____

The Solar System • *Guided Reading and Study*

3. Where has life been found on Earth that suggests life forms may not always need the "Goldilocks conditions"?

_____

_____

_____

_____

Life Elsewhere in the Solar System? (pp. 110–111)

4. Why is Mars the most obvious place to look for living things like those on Earth?

_____

_____

5. Why do scientists hypothesize that Mars may once have had the conditions needed for life to exist?

_____

_____

_____

_____

6. A meteorite from Mars found in Antarctica in 1996 shows tiny shapes that look like _____.

7. Is the following sentence true or false? All scientists agree that the meteorite from Mars shows that life once existed on Mars.

_____

8. Which spacecraft tested the soil of Mars for signs of life?

_____

_____

9. Is the following sentence true or false? Life has been discovered in Martian soil. _____

10. What suggests that there might be liquid water on Europa?

_____

_____

_____

_____

11. Is the following sentence true or false? If there is liquid water on Europa, there might also be life. _____

Name _____ Date _____ Class _____

The Solar System • *Guided Reading and Study*

Is There Life Beyond Earth? *(continued)*

12. Complete the table that compares and contrasts what scientists know and what they hypothesize about life on Mars and on Europa.

	Mars	**Europa**
What Scientists Know So Far	There are surface features that appear to have been formed by liquid water.	It has a smooth, ice crust with cracks.
What Scientists Hypothesize	a.	b.

   c. According to these hypotheses, which location is more likely to have life now?

_____

_____

_____

   d. Based on this table, write a definition of a hypothesis in your own words.

_____

_____

_____

Name _____ Date _____ Class _____

Key Terms

Clues

Answer the questions by writing the correct key terms in the blanks. Use the circled letters to find the hidden key term. Then write a definition for the hidden key term.

1. What is the name of the sun's surface layer?

   _ O _ _ _ _ _ O _ _

2. What is an elongated circle, or oval shape, called?

   _ _ O _ _ _ _

3. What are the objects called that orbit the sun in a belt between Mars and Jupiter?

   _ _ _ _ _ O _ _

4. What is the trapping of heat by the atmosphere?

   _ _ _ _ _ O _ _ _   _ _ _ _ _ _

5. What is a description of the solar system in which all the planets revolve around Earth?

   _ _ _ O _ _ _ _ _

6. What is a chunk of rock or dust in space called?

   _ _ _ O _ _ _ _ _

7. What are reddish loops of gas that connect different parts of sunspot regions?

   _ _ _ _ O _ _ _ _

8. What are areas of gas on the sun that are cooler than the gases around them?

   _ _ _ _ _ O _

9. What is a stream of electrically charged particles sent out by the corona called?

   _ _ _ _ O _ O _ _

10. What is the outer layer of the sun's atmosphere?

    O _ _ _ _ _

Key Term: _ _ _ _ _ _ _ _ _ _ _ _ _ _

Definition:

_____

_____

Stars, Galaxies, and the Universe ▪ *Guided Reading and Study*

Telescopes (pp. 118–124)

This section describes electromagnetic radiation. It also explains how different types of telescopes work and where they are located.

Use Target Reading Skills

The first column in the chart lists key terms in this section. Write what you know about the key term in the second column. As you read, write a definition of the key term in your own words in the third column. Some examples are done for you. Connecting what you already know about key terms helps you to remember them.

Key Term	What You Know	Definition
Telescope	You use it to see distant objects better.	Device that makes distant objects seem closer
Electromagnetic radiation	You can see only some types of it.	Energy that can move through space in the form of waves
Visible light		
Wavelength		
Spectrum		
Optical telescope		
Refracting telescope		
Convex lens		
Reflecting telescope		
Radio telescope		
Observatory		

Stars, Galaxies, and the Universe • *Guided Reading and Study*

Electromagnetic Radiation (p. 119)

1. What is electromagnetic radiation?

   _____

   _____

   _____

2. The light you see with your eyes is called _____.

3. The distance between the crest of one wave and the crest of the next wave is called a(n) _____.

4. A range of light of different colors and different wavelengths is called a(n) _____.

5. What colors form the spectrum of visible light?

   _____

   _____

6. What wavelengths are included in the electromagnetic spectrum?

   _____

   _____

   _____

   _____

Types of Telescopes (pp. 120–121)

7. What do telescopes collect and focus?

   _____

   _____

   _____

8. What is a convex lens?

   _____

   _____

   _____

Stars, Galaxies, and the Universe • *Guided Reading and Study*

Telescopes *(continued)*

9. Complete the table to compare and contrast different types of telescopes.

Telescopes	
Type	**Description**
Refracting telescope	a.
Reflecting telescope	b.
Radio telescope	c.

    d. How is a radio telescope different from both a refracting and a reflecting telescope?

    _____

    _____

    e. How is a radio telescope similar to both a refracting and a reflecting telescope?

    _____

    _____

10. Which telescope uses convex lenses? _____

11. The largest visible light telescopes are now all _____.

Observatories (pp. 122–124)

12. A building that contains one or more telescopes is called a(n) _____.

13. Why have astronomers built the largest optical telescopes on the tops of mountains?

    _____

    _____

    _____

14. Why have astronomers placed telescopes in space?

    _____

    _____

    _____

15. Why can the Hubble Space Telescope make very detailed images in visible light?

    _____

    _____

    _____

    _____

Stars, Galaxies, and the Universe • *Guided Reading and Study*

Characteristics of Stars (pp. 126–133)

This section explains how astronomers measure distances to stars. It also describes how stars are classified.

Use Target Reading Skills

As you read about stars, stop and write what you know about that topic. As you read the section, write what you learn. An example is done for you.

What You Know
1. Stars are bright and hot.
2.
3.

What You Learned
1.
2.
3.

Introduction (p. 126)

1. Imaginary patterns of stars are called _____.

Classifying Stars (pp. 127–128)

2. What are five characteristics used to classify stars?

   a. _____   b. _____

   c. _____   d. _____

   e. _____

3. What reveals a star's surface temperature?

   _____

   _____

Characteristics of Stars *(continued)*

4. Circle the letter of what is revealed by the red color of the supergiant star called Betelgeuse.

    a. It is an extremely hot star.
    b. It is in a constellation.
    c. It is far away.
    d. It is a fairly cool star.

5. Stars that are much larger than the sun are called _____.

6. Is the following sentence true or false? Each element has a unique set of lines on a spectrum. _____

7. How can astronomers infer which elements are found in a star?

    _____

    _____

    _____

    _____

8. What does a spectrograph do?

    _____

    _____

    _____

9. What is the chemical composition of most stars?

    _____

    _____

Brightness of Stars (pp. 128–129)

10. The amount of light a star gives off is called its _____.

11. Why does Rigel shine as brightly as Betelgeuse, even though Rigel is much smaller than Betelgeuse?

    _____

    _____

    _____

    _____

Stars, Galaxies, and the Universe · *Guided Reading and Study*

12. What two factors determine how bright a star looks from Earth?

    a. _____

    b. _____

13. Complete the table about the measurement of a star's brightness.

Brightness of Stars	
Measurement of Brightness	**Definition**
Apparent brightness	a.
Absolute brightness	b.

   Star X is closer to Earth than Star Y. Star X appears brighter than Star Y. Use the table to answer the following questions.

   c. Compare Star X with Star Y using the term *apparent brightness*.

   _____

   _____

   _____

   d. Can you compare the absolute brightness of Star X with Star Y? Why or why not?

   _____

   _____

   _____

   _____

   _____

14. Is the following sentence true or false? The closer a star is to Earth, the brighter it appears. _____

Stars, Galaxies, and the Universe • *Guided Reading and Study*

Characteristics of Stars *(continued)*

15. What two things must an astronomer find out in order to calculate a star's absolute brightness?

a. _____

b. _____

Measuring Distances to Stars (pp. 130–131)

16. Is the following sentence true or false? In space, light travels at a speed of 300,000 kilometers per year. _____

17. What is a light-year?

_____

_____

_____

18. A light-year equals about _____ kilometers.

19. Is the following sentence true or false? The light-year is a unit of time.

_____

20. What is parallax?

_____

_____

_____

21. Astronomers often use parallax to measure the distance to which of the following objects?

a. distant stars
b. the sun
c. the planets
d. nearby stars

22. To measure parallax shift, astronomers look at the same star at two different times of the year, when Earth is on different sides of the _____.

The Hertzsprung-Russell Diagram (pp. 132–133)

23. The diagram that shows the relationship between the surface temperatures of stars and their absolute brightness is called the _____.

24. Look at the Hertzsprung-Russell diagram in your textbook. Write what is measured on each of the two axes of the diagram.

a. *x*-axis (horizontal axis): _____

b. *y*-axis (vertical axis): _____

25. An area on the Hertzsprung-Russell diagram that runs from the upper left to the lower right and includes more than 90 percent of all stars is called the _____.

26. Circle the letter of each sentence that is true based on the Hertzsprung-Russell diagram in your textbook.

    a. The sun is a main-sequence star.

    b. The absoute brightness of white dwarfs is greater than that of supergiants.

    c. Rigel is hotter than Betelgeuse.

    d. The absolute brightness of Polaris is greater than that of the sun.

Stars, Galaxies, and the Universe ▪ *Guided Reading and Study*

Lives of Stars (pp. 136–140)

This section explains how the life of a star begins. It also explains what determines how long a star lives and what happens when a star runs out of fuel.

Use Target Reading Skills

As you read about the stages in the life of a star, make a flowchart that shows the stages in the life of a low-mass star like the sun. The first step is done for you.

Life Cycle of a Sun-Like Star

Protostar forms from a nebula.

↓

a.

↓

b.

↓

c.

The Lives of Stars (p. 137)

1. Is the following sentence true or false? All stars begin their lives as parts of nebulas. _____

2. A large amount of gas and dust spread out in an immense volume is called a(n) _____.

3. A contracting cloud of gas and dust with enough mass to form a star is called a(n) _____.

4. Describe how a star is born.

   _____

   _____

   _____

Stars, Galaxies, and the Universe ▪ *Guided Reading and Study*

5. Circle the letter of the factor that determines how long a star lives.
   a. its mass *pg137*
   b. its brightness
   c. its volume
   d. its temperature

6. Is the following sentence true or false? Stars with more mass last longer than stars with less mass. _____ *pg 137* _____

Deaths of Stars (pp. 138–140)

Match each stage of a star with its definition.

Stage of a Star	Definition
_e_ 7. White dwarf *pg 138*	a. The small, dense remains of a high-mass star that is called a pulsar when it spins
_d_ 8. Planetary nebula *pg 138*	b. Explosion of a high-mass star
_b_ 9. Supernova *pg 139*	c. An object whose gravity is so strong nothing can escape
_a_ 10. Neutron star *pg 139*	d. A glowing cloud of gas formed from the expanding outer layers of a red giant
_c_ 11. Black hole *pg 140*	e. The cooled core of a star that has run out of fuel

12. Complete the flowchart to show the stages in the lives of high-mass stars.

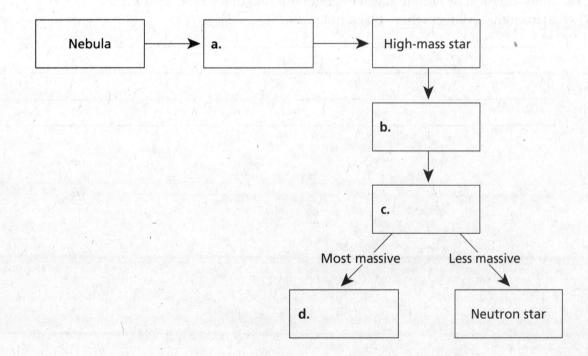

Stars, Galaxies, and the Universe • *Guided Reading and Study*

Lives of Stars *(continued)*

e. What determines which stage occurs after a supernova?

_____

_____

_____

f. How do all stars begin?

_____

_____

g. What is the relationship between mass and the end stages of stars?

_____

_____

_____

_____

_____

_____

13. How do astronomers think the sun may have begun?

_____

_____

_____

14. Since no form of radiation can ever get out of a black hole, how can astronomers detect where black holes are?

_____

_____

_____

_____

Stars, Galaxies, and the Universe · *Guided Reading and Study*

Star Systems and Galaxies (pp. 141–147)

This section explains what a star system is, describes the major types of galaxies, and describes the scale of the universe.

Use Target Reading Skills

The first column in the chart lists key terms in this section. As you read the section, write a definition of the key term in your own words in the second column. Underline the most important feature or function in each definition. An example is done for you.

Key Term	Definition
Binary star	Star system with <u>two stars</u>.
Eclipsing binary	A system in which one star periodically blocks the light from another.
Open cluster	Have a loose disorganized appearance and contain no more than a few thousand stars - often contains many bright supergiants and much gas + dust.
Globular cluster	large groups of older stars. Round and densely packed with stars - may
Galaxy	
Spiral galaxy	
Elliptical galaxy	
Irregular galaxy	
Quasar	
Universe	
Scientific notation	

Stars, Galaxies, and the Universe • *Guided Reading and Study*

Star Systems and Galaxies (continued)

Star Systems and Clusters (pp. 142–143)

1. What are star systems?

   _____

   _____

2. Star systems with two stars are called double stars or _____.

3. How can astronomers tell whether there is an unseen second star in a system?

   a. They observe the effects of its gravity on the brighter star.
   b. They measure the parallax of the second star.
   c. They send a probe to the second star.
   d. They observe regular changes in the brightness of the star system.

4. A star system in which one star periodically blocks the light from another star is a(n) _____.

5. How did astronomers first discover a planet revolving around another star?

   _____

   _____

6. Why have most new planets discovered around other stars been very large?

   _____

   _____

7. A grouping of stars that has a loose, disorganized appearance and contains no more than a few thousand stars is called a(n) _____.

8. A large grouping of stars that contains mostly older stars is called a(n)
   _____.

Galaxies (p. 144)

9. What is a galaxy?

   _____

   _____

Match the type of galaxy with its shape.

Type of Galaxy	Description of Shape
____ 10. Spiral galaxy	a. Bulge in middle and arms that spiral outward
____ 11. Elliptical galaxy	b. Does not have a regular shape
____ 12. Irregular galaxy	c. Looks like round or flattened ball

Stars, Galaxies, and the Universe • *Guided Reading and Study*

13. Circle the letter of each sentence that is true about galaxies.

    a. Elliptical galaxies contain only new stars.

    b. Irregular galaxies usually have many bright, young stars.

    c. In spiral galaxies, most new stars form in the spiral arms.

    d. Quasars have huge bar-shaped regions of stars that pass through their center.

14. A very bright, distant, young galaxy with a giant black hole at the center is called a(n) _____.

The Milky Way (p. 145)

15. The galaxy in which our solar system is located is called the

    _____.

16. What type of galaxy is the Milky Way?

    _____

    _____

    _____

    _____

The Scale of the Universe (pp. 146–147)

17. Why do astronomers often use scientific notation?

    _____

    _____

18. Suppose a star is about 38,000,000,000,000 kilometers away from Earth. How do you write this number in scientific notation?

    _____

    _____

19. What is the Local Group?

    _____

    _____

20. How large is the observable universe? _____

Name _____ Date _____ Class _____

The Expanding Universe (pp. 148–153)

This section explains how astronomers think the universe and the solar system formed.

Use Target Reading Skills

As you read about the evidence that supports the big bang theory, complete the graphic organizer.

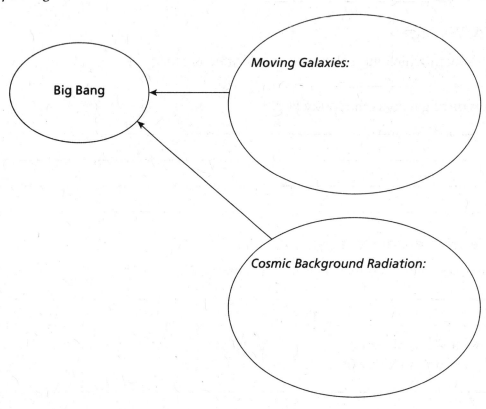

Big Bang

Moving Galaxies:

Cosmic Background Radiation:

How the Universe Formed (pp. 148–150)

1. The initial explosion that resulted in the formation and expansion of the universe is called the _____.

2. When did the big bang occur?

   _____

3. Is the following sentence true or false? The farther away a galaxy is from us, the faster it is moving away from us. _____

4. How is the universe like rising raisin bread dough?

   _____

   _____

   _____

   _____

Name _____ Date _____ Class _____

Stars, Galaxies, and the Universe • *Guided Reading and Study*

5. Radiation left over from the big bang is called _____.

6. How can astronomers infer approximately how long the universe has been expanding?

_____

_____

Formation of the Solar System (p. 151)

7. About how long ago did our solar system form? _____

8. What events led to the birth of the sun?

_____

_____

_____

_____

_____

9. How did planetesimals form planets?

_____

_____

_____

The Future of the Universe (p. 152)

10. Describe two possibilities of what will happen to the universe in the future.

a. _____

_____

_____

_____

b. _____

_____

_____

_____

_____

11. Which possibility in question 10 is more likely? Explain why.

_____

_____

_____

_____

Key Terms

Solve the clues by filling in the blanks with key terms from the chapter. Then write the numbered letters in the correct order to find the hidden message.

Clues   **Key Terms**

1. The earliest stage of a star's life
    _ _ _ _ _ _ _ _
          1

2. An object with gravity so strong nothing can escape
    _ _ _ _ _ _ _ _ _
          2

3. An instrument that breaks the light from an object
    into colors
    _ _ _ _ _ _ _ _ _ _
      3

4. All of space and everything in it
    _ _ _ _ _ _ _ _
         4

5. The small, dense remains of a high-mass star
    _ _ _ _ _ _ _ _ _ _
      5

6. The explosion that formed the universe
    _ _ _ _ _ _ _
         6

7. A pattern of stars in the sky
    _ _ _ _ _ _ _ _ _ _ _ _
            7

8. The explosion of a dying giant or supergiant star
    _ _ _ _ _ _ _ _
    8

9. A galaxy that has a pinwheel shape
    _ _ _ _ _ _ _ _ _ _
        9

10. A building that contains one or more telescopes
    _ _ _ _ _ _ _ _ _ _
     10

11. A device used to detect radio waves from
    objects in space
    _ _ _ _ _ _ _ _ _ _ _ _
          11

12. The apparent change in position of an object when
    you look at it from different places
    _ _ _ _ _ _ _
      12

13. A distant galaxy with a black hole at its center
    _ _ _ _ _ _
       13

Hidden Message

_ _ _ _ _ _ _ _ _ _ _ _ _ .
1 2 3 4 5 6 7 8 9 10 11 12 13